EASY GO-TO EVERYDAY RECIPES

IN THE
BOWL

MICHELLE COUGHRAN

Introduction

Alright yall... Tonight for dinner is... One of the amazing and simple recipes in this book, from yours truly. "Put it in the bowl". I am beyond excited and grateful you have chosen my easy recipes and book to have in your house, so let's get to cooking.

I do not want you to feel overwhelmed and hopefully with my easy go-to recipes we can accomplish that goal. I do not do neutral, I do loud, delicious, flavorful and easy recipes. We love to measure with our hearts in our house and we have big hearts, so I would highly suggest taking all my measurements with caution (mainly seasonings). I worked very hard to bring you the most flavorful, easiest and affordable recipes that even my picky kids enjoy. Every dish has been tested and approved by my amazing family and friends that honestly are just as picky as my children.

My goal with this book is to help take some of the stress off of those busy adults. I've tried my hardest to ensure the instructions on each recipe are very easy to understand and straight to the point. Some of the recipes have notes on them to give extra advice on some of the dishes (if needed of course). I am so excited to bring you my recipes and hope you enjoy them as much as we do.

Contents

Dips

In this chapter you will find easy, and simple dips that are full of flavor. These simple dips are great for any occasion and I hope you enjoy them as much as I do!

Taco Dip

INGREDIENTS

1-15.25oz can of corn (drained)

1-10oz can of Rotel (drained)

1 packet of Ranch seasoning

1 packet of Taco seasoning

½ Cup mayonnaise

½ Cup sour cream

1 Cup shredded cheese

DIRECTIONS

1. Place all ingredients in a bowl and mix well.

2. Cover and place in the refrigerator and let sit for at least 1 hour before serving.

Notes: *Best if served with Tortilla Chips or Doritos©.*

Jalapeno Popper Dip

INGREDIENTS

1 block cream cheese (softened)

1 cup sour cream

1 cup bacon bits

1 packet Ranch seasoning

1-10oz can Rotel (drained)

2 tbsp fresh minced garlic

½ cup sharp Cheddar cheese

½ cup Pepper Jack cheese

5 whole Jalapenos

DIRECTIONS

1. Slice the Jalapenos in half and take the seeds out.
2. Dice the Jalapenos up into small pieces.
3. Place Jalapenos and the rest of the ingredients in a bowl and mix well.
4. Cover with lid and place in the refrigerator for 1 hour before serving.

Notes: Best served with Tortilla Chips or Crackers.

Fajita Dip

INGREDIENTS

1 lb ground beef

1 yellow bell pepper

1 red bell pepper

1 green bell pepper

1-15.25oz can of corn (drained)

1 cup sharp Cheddar cheese

1 cup Pepper Jack Cheese

1 cup sour cream

1 cup mayonnaise

1 packet Fajita seasoning

½ yellow onion

3 tbsp butter

DIRECTIONS

1. Chop bell peppers and onion.

2. Melt butter in a pan and cook bell peppers and onions until soft.

3. Once the peppers and onions are soft, put your ground beef and minced garlic into the same pan and cook until done.

4. Place cooked ground beef and peppers into a mixing bowl.

5. Add the rest of the ingredients listed and mix well.

6. Serve and enjoy!

Notes: Can eat dip warm or chilled.
Best served with Tortilla Chips or Frito® Scoops®.

Dill Pickle Dip

INGREDIENTS

1 block cream cheese (softened)

1 cup sour cream

1 packet Ranch seasoning

½ cup fresh dill (chopped)

½ cup fresh chives (chopped)

10 petite dill pickles (chopped)

1 tbsp minced garlic

1 tbsp pickle juice

½ cup bacon bits

DIRECTIONS

1. Finely chop fresh dill, chives and Petite dill pickles.
2. Place the dill, chives and pickles with the rest of the ingredients in a bowl.
3. Mix all ingredients until well combined.
4. Cover and place in the refrigerator for 1 hour before serving.

Notes: Best served with Lays© Potato Chips or Vegetables!

Sides

In this Chapter, you will see a couple of my favorite side dishes that go great with any main dish. These simple side dishes are not just your average everyday sides and will help give you some other options to bring to your table.

Brussel Sprouts

INGREDIENTS

1 Bag of Brussel sprouts

1 tsp pepper

1 tsp salt

1 tsp of oregano

1 tsp of crushed red pepper flakes

1 tbsp of paprika

1 tbsp of garlic powder

2 tbsp of olive oil

GLAZE INGREDIENTS

2 tbsp of stick butter

¼ cup maple syrup

½ tsp crushed red pepper flakes

½ tsp Italian seasoning

½ tsp garlic powder

DIRECTIONS

1. Preheat oven to 400°F.
2. Take wilted leaves off of the Brussel sprouts.
3. Rinse them and place in a bowl.
4. Coat them heavily with olive oil and salt.
5. In a pot, boil water and place Brussel sprouts in the pot once water is boiling. Cook Brussel sprouts in boiling water for 5 mins. Drain the sprouts and place in an ice bath for another 5 mins.
6. While sprouts are cooling, preheat your oven to 400°F and get a cooking sheet, drizzle olive oil all over it and place in the oven while its preheating.
7. After the sprouts are cooled, slice them in half and place in a bowl.
8. Season them with olive oil, salt, pepper, oregano, crushed red pepper flakes, paprika and garlic powder. Mix well so the sprouts are coated evenly.
9. Take sprouts and place face down, skin side up on a cooking sheet, and bake at 400°F for 25 minutes.
10. Top with glaze.

GLAZE INSTRUCTIONS

1. In a small microwavable bowl, take 2 tbsp butter, ½ cup maple syrup, 1/2 tsp crushed red pepper flakes, ½ tsp of Italian seasoning, and ½ tsp garlic powder.
2. Place in the microwave for 1 min or until butter is melted and mix well.
3. Let sit for 2 to 3 minutes.
4. Pour over sprouts and enjoy!

Extra Mac N Cheese

INGREDIENTS

1 box Velveeta© Mac N Cheese

2 cups bacon

3 tbsp butter

1 block cream cheese (softened)

½ cup sour cream

1 cup heavy whipping cream

1 cup Mozzarella cheese

1 cup green onion

DIRECTIONS

1. Preheat oven to 375°F.

2. Cook noodles according to directions on the box and set aside the Velveeta© Cheese Packet. It is very important that you do not overcook your noodles.

3. Take 6 slices of bacon, and chop them up into small pieces. Cook bacon until done and crispy.

4. In a baking dish, put cooked noodles, Velveeta© Sauce Packet, Butter, Cream Cheese, Sour Cream, Heavy Whipping Cream, and half of the cooked chopped up Bacon. Mix until all is well combined in the baking dish.

5. Top with Mozzarella Cheese, cover with foil and bake in the oven at 375°F for 20 minutes.

6. Once it is done baking in the oven, top with the rest of chopped up Bacon and Green Onion.

7. Let sit for 10 mins before serving and enjoy!

Sausage Balls

INGREDIENTS

1 lb Great Value© sausage

1 lb cheddar cheese

3 cups Bisquick©

DIRECTIONS

1. Preheat oven to 350°F.
2. Combine all ingredients into a large bowl.
3. Shape into pucks or balls.
4. Bake at 350°F for 15 - 20 minutes.

Notes: This recipe has been in my family since before I was born and we make them every year to eat on Christmas morning, but is great for a side dish or easy breakfast on the go meal.
Makes roughly 50 Sausage Balls .

Jalapeno Popper Pigs In A Blanket

INGREDIENTS

8 whole Jalapenos

1 package of Lit'l Smokies©

1 block cream cheese (Softened)

1 cup Colby Jack Shredded cheese

1 cup bacon

2 Of The 8 Count Crescent Rolls

1 packet of Dry Ranch seasoning

DIRECTIONS

1. Preheat oven at 400°F.
2. Chop up bacon into small pieces and cook.
3. Slice jalapenos in half and take the seeds out.
4. In a mixing bowl, combine cream cheese, bacon, shredded cheese and Dry Ranch seasoning.
5. Take the cream cheese mixture and place a spoonful into each jalapeno half.
6. Once each jalapeno half is filled, place 1 Lit'l Smokie© onto each jalapeno.
7. Place jalapeno onto a crescent slice and roll.
8. Bake in the oven at 400°F for 18 mins or until the peppers are soft and the crescent is golden brown. Air frying is also a cooking option - air fry at 375°F for 8-10 minutes.

Mozzarella Onion Rings

INGREDIENTS

1 large yellow onion

1 package of sliced Mozzarella Cheese

2 cups of flour

2 large white eggs

1 cup milk

2 cups cooking oil

Italian Panko breadcrumbs

DIRECTIONS

1. Slice onion and pull apart the rings into various sizes.

2. Place the smaller ring into a bigger ring, leaving enough room in between the rings for the cheese slice.

3. Take sliced Mozzarella cheese and cut into thin strips.

4. Place thin cut cheese strips in between the smaller and larger rings.

5. Set in the freezer for 15 minutes which will make breading easier. Meanwhile mix the eggs and milk together.

6. Place rings into the flour first covering the entire thing, then dipping them into the egg and milk mixture. After that place them in the breadcrumbs, coating the entire ring and setting aside to rest.

7. Heat cooking oil to no more than 350°F.

8. Place rings into cooking oil for 3-4 minutes each side.

9. Once rings are cooked let sit for 5 minutes before serving and enjoy.

Loaded Hash Browns

INGREDIENTS

Frozen Hash Brown patties

Dean's Creamy Dill Dip©

Colby Jack shredded cheese

Bacon

Sour cream

Green onion

DIRECTIONS

1. Preheat Oven to 400°F.

2. Cook frozen hash brown patties according to package directions, flipping halfway through cook time.

3. Cut up bacon into small pieces and cook until crispy.

4. Place a scoop of the Dean's Creamy Dill Dip© onto each one of the cooked hash brown patties and spread evenly.

5. Next place shredded cheese and cooked bacon pieces onto each hash brown patties.

6. Place hash brown patties back into a 400°F oven for 8 mins to melt the cheese.

7. Top with green onion and sour cream.

8. Serve and enjoy!

Easy Meals

In this chapter you will find the easiest, most flavorful, and affordable main dish ideas to feed your family. Let me help you get dinner on the table with minimum effort and a taste that will have you coming back for more!

Mexican Chicken

INGREDIENTS

3 boneless, skinless chicken breasts (shredded)

1 10.5oz can Cream of Chicken soup

1 10.5oz can Cream of Mushroom soup

1-10oz can Rotel (drained)

1 cup sour cream

1 package of Taco seasoning

1 family size bag of Doritos©

1 8oz block of Colby Jack cheese (shredded)

½ Yellow onion (diced)

DIRECTIONS

1. Preheat oven to 375°F.

2. Cook chicken breasts until internal temp reaches 165°F. Once the chicken is fully cooked then shred.

3. Shred the entire 8oz block of Colby Jack cheese. Note: you can use pre-shredded cheese.

4. In a large bowl combine the shredded chicken, can of cream of chicken, cream of mushroom, Rotel, sour cream, diced onions and Taco seasoning. Mix until all ingredients are well combined.

5. Crush the entire bag of Doritos©.

6. In a baking dish layer up the ingredients, starting with the crushed Doritos© on the bottom, then a thin layer of the chicken mixture and top with the shredded cheese. Repeat the process, ensuring you have at least two layers of the chicken. When you get to the final layer of the cheese, place another light layer of the crushed Doritos© on the top.

7. Cover with foil and place in oven at 375°F for 20 minutes.

8. Uncover and place back in the oven for an additional 5 minutes.

9. Let sit for 5-7 minutes before serving and enjoy!

Doritos Casserole

INGREDIENTS

1½ lb ground beef

1-8oz block Colby Jack cheese (shredded)

1-10oz can Rotel (drained)

1-10.5oz can Cream of Chicken soup

1-10.5oz can Cream of Chicken With Herb soup

1 yellow onion (diced)

1 tbsp of minced garlic

1 packet of Taco seasoning

1 packet of Ranch seasoning

1-14½oz bag of Doritos©

DIRECTIONS

1. Preheat Oven to 375°F.

2. In a skillet combine ground beef, diced onion and garlic. Cook until ground beef is cooked fully and onions are soft.

3. In a large mixing bowl, combine cooked ground beef, shredded cheese, Cream of Chicken, Cream of Chicken with Herbs, Rotel, Taco seasoning and Ranch seasoning and mix well.

4. Crush the Doritos© in the bag.

5. In a baking dish, put a layer of crushed Doritos© on the bottom of the dish. Place half of the meat mixture over the crushed Doritos© and top with shredded cheese. Then repeat the layering process again.

6. Top with a little bit more of the crushed Doritos© and shredded cheese.

7. Cover with foil and bake at 375°F for 25 minutes.

8. Let rest for 5-7 minutes before serving and enjoy!

Cheesy Beef Enchiladas

INGREDIENTS

1 lb ground beef

1- 10oz can of Rotel

1-10.5oz can of refried beans

2 cups shredded cheese

1 Packet of Taco seasoning

2- 10oz cans of Red Enchilada sauce

Flour tortillas

DIRECTIONS

1. Preheat oven to 350°F.

2. In a skillet cook ground beef and drain the grease. In the same skillet with the drained ground beef add in Taco seasoning, Rotel, refried beans, 1 Cup of shredded cheese and half of a can of the Enchilada sauce. Mix until well combined and let simmer for 10 minutes covered.

3. In a baking dish, pour the rest of the opened can of Red Enchilada Sauce in the bottom of the dish covering the bottom evenly.

4. Place meat mixture inside the flour tortilla and roll up like a burrito. Place your filled rolled tortillas on top of the Red Enchilada Sauce in the baking dish.

5. Top with the last full can of Red Enchilada sauce and shredded cheese.

6. Cover and bake at 350°F for 25 minutes.

7. Let rest for 7 minutes before serving and enjoy!

Memaw's Enchiladas

INGREDIENTS

1 rotisserie chicken (chopped)

1 10.5oz can Cream of Mushroom soup

1 block cream cheese (softened)

1 stick butter

½ yellow onion (diced)

⅓ cup milk

⅓ cup sour cream

2 cups shredded cheese

1 tbps minced garlic

1 tbsp pepper

Flour tortillas

DIRECTIONS

1. Preheat Oven to 375°F.

2. Melt your stick of butter in a pan and place diced onion into melted butter, cooking them until soft.

3. Place chopped rotisserie chicken, cream cheese, sour cream, minced garlic and pepper into a pan with your soft cooked onions. Mix well until everything is melted down and well combined.

4. Fill tortillas with chicken mixture, roll up like a burrito and place in a baking dish.

5. In a separate bowl, combine Cream of Mushroom and milk.

6. Pour Cream of Mushroom and milk mixture over the top of filled tortillas in a baking dish.

7. Top with shredded cheese and cover with foil.

8. Bake In oven at 375°F for 25 minutes.

9. Serve and enjoy!

Heart Attack Patties

INGREDIENTS

6 pre-made hamburger patties

1 packet of Lipton© Beefy onion Soup Packet

1- 8oz block of Colby Jack cheese (Shredded)

2 - 10.5oz cans of Cream of Mushroom with Roasted Garlic soup

Worcestershire Sauce

Kinders© Buttery Steakhouse seasoning

DIRECTIONS

1. Preheat oven to 375°F.
2. Season pre-made hamburger patties with Worcestershire Sauce and Kinders© Buttery Steakhouse seasoning on both sides.
3. Cook hamburgers to your liking.
4. Shred the block of Colby Jack cheese.
5. In a baking dish spread out one can of the Cream of Mushroom with Roasted Garlic in the bottom of the dish.
6. Spread half the packet of the Lipton© Beefy Onion Soup Mix over the Cream of Mushroom with Roasted Garlic.
7. Place cooked hamburger patties in a baking dish over the Cream of Mushroom with Roasted Garlic and Lipton© Beefy Onion Soup Mix Packet.
8. Take the last can of Cream of Mushroom with Roasted Garlic and place over the top of the patties, covering each one fully. Next take the rest of your Lipton© Beefy Onion Soup Mix and sprinkle over the top of the hamburgers covered in the Cream of Mushroom with Roasted Garlic.
9. Top with shredded Cheese and cover with foil.
10. Bake at 375°F for 25 minutes.
11. Serve and enjoy!

Goulash

INGREDIENTS

1-16oz box elbow pasta

1-10.5oz can tomato sauce

1½ tbsp tomato paste

1-10.5oz can corn (drained)

1-10oz can Rotel (drained)

1 lb ground beef

Kinder's© The Blend

Italian seasoning

1 tbsp minced garlic

Parsley

Onion powder

DIRECTIONS

1. Cook elbow pasta and drain water.

2. Cook ground beef, then season with Kinder's© The Blend, Italian seasoning and parsley. Drain grease and add can of drained corn, can of drained Rotel, can of tomato sauce and tomato paste and let simmer for 10 minutes.

3. Combine cooked and drained pasta noodles with meat mixture. Ensure it is mixed very well!

4. Serve and Enjoy!

Loaded Brisket Baked Potato

INGREDIENTS

Brisket (size varies)

Sriracha sauce

Mustard

White Queso

Tomato

Onion

Chives

BBQ sauce

Sour cream

Whole potatoes

Shredded cheese

Carne Asada seasoning

DIRECTIONS

1. Lay brisket out on a covered surface.

2. Cover brisket in equal parts of Sriracha sauce and mustard.

3. Season brisket with Carne Asada seasoning, ensuring the entire brisket is covered. Cook until brisket reaches internal temp of 195°F. Can cook in a slow cooker on high for 4-5 Hours, or on the smoker.

4. Wash and poke holes into the whole potatoes placing them on a plate. Cook in the microwave for 12 minutes or until potatoes are fork tender for a fast and easy cooking method.

5. Shred brisket.

6. Slice open cooked potato and loosen up the inside of the potato.

7. Place shredded cheese, desired amount of shredded brisket, and White Queso sauce over the potato.

8. Top with your favorite toppings (we like to top ours with tomato, onion and chives).

9. Drizzle BBQ sauce and sour cream.

10. Serve and enjoy!

A.C.P

INGREDIENTS

1 lb chicken breasts (boneless/skinless)

3 cups instant white rice

1⅓ tbsp Knorr© Tomato Bouillon With Chicken Flavor

White Queso

½ Stick of butter

1 tbsp minced garlic

1 packet of Fajita seasoning

DIRECTIONS

1. Slice up chicken breasts into strips and place in skillet with butter, minced garlic and Fajita seasoning. Cook until chicken reaches internal temp of 165°F.

2. In a microwavable safe bowl, add Instant rice and tomato bouillon. Cook rice according to directions on the box.

3. Layer your plate, placing cooked rice first, then place your cooked chicken on top of the bed of rice.

4. Top with White Queso and enjoy!

Notes: An addition to your dish, you can add a scoop of cooked refried beans to the plate as well and eat on a warm tortilla or scoop with tortilla chips!

Chicken and Rice

INGREDIENTS

3 chicken breasts (cubed)

2 packages of the Knorr© Chicken Flavor Broccoli Rice

1-10.5oz can of cream of chicken with herb soup

1-10.5oz can of cream of mushroom with roasted garlic soup

2 cups chicken broth

Kinders© The Blend

Smoked paprika

Shredded cheese

DIRECTIONS

1. Preheat oven to 400°F.

2. In a baking dish, pour both packages of rice, Cream of Chicken with Herb, Cream of Mushroom with Roasted Garlic and Chicken Broth. Mix ingredients together very well.

3. Cube up your chicken breasts and season with Kinders© The Blend and smoked paprika.

4. Place your cubed up chicken on top of the rice in the baking dish pressing them lightly down, but NOT fully submerged.

5. Top with shredded cheese and cover with foil.

6. Bake at 400°F for 35 minutes.

7. Let sit for 5-7 minutes before serving and enjoy!

Mississippi Potatoes

INGREDIENTS

5 large yellow potatoes

2- 14oz Kielbasa Smoked Sausage

1 block cream cheese

1 tbsp Kinder's© Garlic Blend seasoning

1 tbsp pepper

8oz block Colby Jack Cheese

1 tbsp minced garlic

2 sticks of Kerrygold© Garlic and Herb butter

DIRECTIONS

1. Preheat oven 400°F.
2. Chop up your potatoes.
3. Slice Up the Kielbasa Smoked Sausage.
4. In a baking dish place potatoes, Kielbasa Smoked Sausage, garlic blend seasoning, pepper and minced garlic.
5. Shred block of Colby Jack Cheese (can use pre-shredded cheese, I just prefer to shred my own in this recipe as it melts better in my opinion).
6. Cut up block of cream cheese into cubes.
7. Slice up your sticks of Kerrygold© Garlic and Herb butter.
8. Place cream cheese and butter over the top of the potatoes and sausage in the baking dish, making sure to spread out evenly.
9. Cover with foil and bake in oven at 400°F for 1 hour.
10. Remove foil and mix very well ensuring all ingredients are well combined.
11. Top with shredded Colby Jack Cheese and place back in the oven uncovered for an additional 10 minutes.
12. Let sit for 5-7 minutes before serving and enjoy!

Chicken Bacon Ranch Pasta

INGREDIENTS

1 rotisserie chicken (shredded)

1lb box of penne pasta noodles

22oz jar of garlic Parmesan Alfredo sauce

1½ cups heavy whipping cream

3 cups bacon

½ cup onion (diced)

1 tbsp minced garlic

2 packets Ranch seasoning

1 tbsp pepper

1lb block Mozzarella cheese (shredded)

1 cup pre-shredded Parmesan

2 tbs parsley

DIRECTIONS

1. Preheat oven at 375°F.

2. De-bone and shred chicken.

3. Cook pasta noodles according to package instructions.

4. Cut up bacon into small pieces and cook until crispy. Remove from the pan leaving the bacon grease.

5. Place diced onions into bacon grease, adding in minced garlic and cook until soft.

6. In a baking dish place cooked/drained pasta noodles, shredded chicken, jar of Garlic Parmesan Alfredo Sauce, heavy whipping cream, half of your crumbled cooked bacon, cooked onions, 2 packets of Ranch seasoning and pepper. Mix very well until all ingredients are well combined.

7. Top with shredded Mozzarella and Parmesan.

8. Cover with foil and place in oven at 375°F for 25 minutes.

9. Uncover and top with remaining bacon pieces and Parsley.

10. Let sit for 5-7 minutes before serving and enjoy!

Cowboy Pasta

INGREDIENTS

1 lb steak (Sirloin or Ribeye)

8oz Rotini pasta

2 tbsp olive oil

½ cup BBQ sauce

½ cup Ranch dressing

1 cup heavy whipping cream

½ cup Mozzarella cheese

Salt (to taste)

Pepper (to taste)

2 tbsp green onions

1 tbsp Kinder's© Buttery garlic salt

DIRECTIONS

1. Cut steak into strips.

2. Cook pasta according to directions on the package.

3. In a large skillet, heat olive oil over medium heat.

4. Add steak into the skillet with the oil. Season with salt, pepper and Kinder's© Buttery Garlic. Sear for 3-4 minutes until cooked to your liking.

5. Remove the steak from the pan leaving the drippings and reduce your heat to low. Add in BBQ sauce, Ranch dressing and heavy whipping cream. Stir until well combined, but not letting it bubble.

6. Place drained/cooked pasta noodles into the sauce and add Mozzarella. Mix well until everything is combined evenly.

7. Top noodles with cooked steak and green onions.

8. Serve and enjoy!

Honey Garlic Chicken Parm

INGREDIENTS

3-4 boneless skinless chicken breasts

2 tbsp Kinder's© The Blend

2 tbsp smoked paprika

1 tbsp pepper

3 tbsp butter

3 tbsp olive oil

16oz Rotini pasta

⅓ cup honey

1 tbsp soy sauce

1 tbsp minced garlic

2 cups heavy whipping cream

5oz Parmesan cheese

2 tbsp crushed red pepper flakes

2 tbsp parsley

DIRECTIONS

1. Cube up the chicken breasts and place in the large mixing bowl.
2. In the bowl, season the chicken with Kinder's© The Blend, smoked paprika, pepper and olive oil. Mix until all chicken is well coated.
3. Cook pasta according to the directions on the package.
4. In a large skillet, melt butter and add seasoned chicken. Then cook chicken until completely done.
5. In the same skillet as cooked chicken, add honey, soy sauce, minced garlic, heavy whipping cream and Parmesan cheese. Mix until well combined.
6. Combine cooked/drained pasta noodles into the chicken sauce mixture and mix well.
7. Top with crushed red pepper flakes and parsley.
8. Serve and enjoy!

French Onion Pork Chops

INGREDIENTS

6-7 Boneless pork chops

1 cup sour cream

1 Packet of Lipton© Onion Soup Mix

Shredded cheese

Kinder's© The Blend seasoning

Smoked paprika

Crispy fried onions

Bacon bits

DIRECTIONS

1. Preheat Oven to 400°F.

2. Place pork chops in a baking dish and season with Kinder's© The Blend and smoked paprika. Ensure both sides of the pork chops are seasoned.

3. In a small bowl, mix together sour cream and the onion soup mix.

4. Pour mixture over the top of the pork chops, making sure they are covered.

5. Top with shredded cheese, bacon, and crispy fried onions.

6. Cover with foil and bake at 400°F for 30-35 minutes.

7. Serve and enjoy!

Notes: Best Served Over Mash Potatoes.
Can also use regular Bacon, Cooked and Crumbled.

Unicorn Chicken

INGREDIENTS

Chicken legs

11oz box of Fruity Pebbles

1 large egg

1 ½ cups milk

2 cups flour

Salt

Pepper

Garlic salt

Cooking oil

DIRECTIONS

1. Heat cooking oil to 350°F.
2. Pat chicken legs dry and season on both sides with salt, pepper and garlic salt.
3. Place flour on a plate and lightly season with garlic salt, pepper and salt.
4. Crush the bag of Fruity Pebbles and place on a separate plate.
5. In a bowl mix together the milk and egg.
6. Batter the chicken legs starting with flour first, then dip the chicken leg into the egg mixture, and lastly coat the chicken in the Fruity Pebbles, ensuring the entire leg is covered in the cereal. Place on a baking rack for at least 10 minutes in the fridge before frying.
7. Heat the cooking oil and then gently place the chicken legs in the oil, be careful not to overcrowd the pan. Make sure you rotate the legs regularly to ensure the cereal doesn't burn before they are fully cooked.
8. Cook the chicken legs until internal temp reaches 165°F.
9. Serve and enjoy!

Notes: Can Bake in the oven as well at 425°F for 35-40 minutes or internal temp reaches 165°F. Make sure to flip chicken legs in the oven half way through cook time.

Dynamite Bombs

INGREDIENTS

1 lb ground beef

1 lb sausage (original or hot)

2 large eggs

1 block cream cheese (softened)

8oz block sharp Cheddar cheese

1 cup bacon bits

(OPTIONAL) WHITE SAUCE INGREDIENTS

½ block cream cheese

½ cup heavy whipping cream

Dry Ranch seasoning to taste

DIRECTIONS

1. Preheat oven to 375°F.
2. In a large bowl combine ground beef, sausage, eggs, cream cheese, sharp Cheddar cheese and bacon bits, smashing the ingredients very well together.
3. Once mixed together, take a scoop of the meat mixture and form them into golf ball size balls, placing them into rows on a baking sheet.
4. Bake in oven at 375°F for 35 Minutes or until internal temp reaches 160°F.
5. Drizzle white sauce over the top if you choose to make it, and enjoy!

WHITE SAUCE DIRECTIONS

1. Place cream cheese and heavy whipping cream in a pan. Heat it up on the stove on low. Very important to not let it bubble.
2. Once cream cheese is melted and mixed well with the heavy whipping cream add in Dry Ranch seasoning to taste.
3. Let sit for 3-4 minutes before drizzling over the Dynamite Bombs.

Egg Roll In A Bowl

INGREDIENTS

1lb bag of tricolor coleslaw

1lb ground beef

1 tbsp minced garlic

½ yellow onion (chopped)

Chives

2 tbsp soy sauce

Thai style sweet chili sauce

Sesame seeds

DIRECTIONS

1. Cook ground beef with onion, minced garlic and soy sauce.

2. Once ground beef is cooked, drain the grease and add in the bag of coleslaw. Let cook down until soft.

3. Top with desired amount of sesame seeds, Thai Style sweet chili sauce and chives.

Cheesy Taco Rice Bake

INGREDIENTS

1lb ground beef

1 package of Taco seasoning

1 tbsp minced garlic

1-15oz can chili beans

1-15.25oz can corn (drained)

1 Package of Spanish style rice

Shredded cheese

1-10.5oz can refried beans

DIRECTIONS

1. Preheat oven at 375°F.

2. Cook the ground beef, seasoning with Taco seasoning and minced garlic.

3. Cook Spanish style rice.

4. In a large mixing bowl, combine ground beef, corn, chili beans and the rice.

5. In a baking pan spread out refried beans in an even layer on the bottom. Next place meat mixture over the top and cover with shredded cheese.

6. Cover with foil and bake in the oven at 375°F for 30 minutes.

7. Let sit for 5-7 minutes before serving and enjoy!

Cornflake Chicken

INGREDIENTS

3-4 cans of chicken breast

22oz can of Cream of Chicken soup

1 stick of butter (melted)

½ cup of sour cream

1 box of cornflakes cereal (Original)

1 package of Ready Rice roasted chicken

2 cups shredded cheese

12oz bag broccoli florets (frozen/fresh)

1 tbsp minced garlic

1 tbsp Creole seasoning

1 tbsp Kinder's© The Blend

DIRECTIONS

1. Preheat oven to 375°F.

2. In large mixing bowl combine cans of chicken, Kinder's© The Blend, Creole seasoning, minced garlic, Cream of Chicken, sour cream, rice, shredded cheese and broccoli and mix together well, ensure everything is evenly coated in the seasoning

3. Place mixture into a baking dish and top with Cornflakes.

4. Melt butter in a microwavable safe bowl and pour over the top of the Cornflakes.

5. Cover with foil and bake for 375°F for 30 minutes.

6. Let sit for 5-7 minutes before serving and enjoy!

Taco Salad

INGREDIENTS

1 bag of Fritos©

1-15oz Ranch style beans©

Lettuce

Tomato

Onion

Shredded cheese

Catalina dressing

Ground beef (optional)

DIRECTIONS

1. Crush up the bag of Fritos©.

2. Place the desired amount of crushed Fritos© in a serving bowl and top with your favorite salad toppings. (Our family likes lettuce, tomato, onion).

3. Open your can of Ranch Style Beans© and scoop right out of the can desired amount of beans on top of salad toppings. You will NOT warm these up at all or drain the juice. (Trust the process).

4. Top with shredded cheese and Catalina dressing.

Notes: Can Cook Ground Beef and add to Taco Salad as well!

Stuffed Bell Peppers

INGREDIENTS

3 large green bell peppers

1 lb ground beef

1 block cream cheese

1-10oz can Rotel (drained)

1 tbsp minced garlic

1 tbsp Creole seasoning

1 tbsp Kinder's© The Blend

Pepper Jack shredded cheese

DIRECTIONS

1. Preheat oven at 375°F.

2. Slice bell peppers in half and take the seeds out.

3. Cook ground beef and season with minced garlic, Kinder's© The Blend and Creole seasoning.

4. Once ground beef is cooked, drain the grease. Then add in Rotel and cream cheese into the skillet. Let simmer until everything is melted down and well combined.

5. Place a scoop of meat mixture into each half of the bell pepper and top with shredded Pepper Jack cheese.

6. Bake in the oven at 375°F for 35 minutes.

7. Serve and enjoy!

Chicken Quesadillas

INGREDIENTS

Flour tortillas

1 rotisserie chicken (shredded)

1 cup sour cream

1 cup Chipotle sauce

Mozzarella cheese

Sharp Cheddar cheese

DIRECTIONS

1. De-bone and shred up chicken,

2. In a small mixing bowl, combine sour cream and Chipotle sauce.

3. Warm up tortillas in the microwave for 30 seconds to 1 minute.

4. Spread cream sauce over the entire tortilla.

5. Place Mozzarella and sharp Cheddar on one side of the tortilla.

6. Next place the shredded chicken on top of the cheese and top with more sharp cheddar cheese and Mozzarella. Fold the tortilla over, closing it up.

7. Toast both sides of the tortilla in a skillet ensuring the cheese is melted and you have a pretty golden color on both sides of the tortilla.

8. Top with remaining cream sauce and enjoy!

Italian Chicken

INGREDIENTS

2-4 lb chicken thighs (boneless/skinless)

1-15oz bottle of Italian dressing

1 tbsp minced garlic

1 tbsp onion powder

1 tbsp garlic powder

1 tbsp smoked paprika

1 tbsp olive oil

Gallon size bag

DIRECTIONS

1. Prep your chicken thighs, removing the fatty pieces you don't want to eat.

2. Pat chicken thighs dry and place them in the gallon size bag.

3. Pour the entire bottle of Italian dressing into the bag, over the chicken.

4. Add the minced garlic, onion powder, garlic powder and smoked paprika to the bag.

5. Close the bag and shake very well ensuring all the seasonings are mixed well. Place the bag in the refrigerator for 2 hours to marinate.

6. Heat the skillet with olive oil and then add the chicken thighs, cooking until the internal temp reaches 165°F.

7. Serve and enjoy!

Poor Boy Pies

INGREDIENTS

2-12.5oz cans chunk chicken breast

1-8ct. biscuits

2 cups shredded cheese

1 cup sour cream

2 tbsp Kinder's© Garlic and Herb seasoning

Spray olive oil

Garlic salt

1 package of Dry Ranch seasoning

DIRECTIONS

1. Drain the water out of the can of chicken and pour the chicken in a skillet. Drizzle a little bit of cooking oil over top of chicken and cook on medium to high heat.

2. Season the chicken breast chunks with the garlic and herb seasoning.

3. Once the chicken is heated and sizzling, add the sour cream, dry ranch seasoning and shredded cheese. Mix until everything is evenly combined together.

4. Roll out biscuits flat with a rolling pin and place a scoop of the chicken mixture on one side of the biscuits (make sure to leave room on the edges) and fold over like a pocket. Press the edges together with a fork.

5. Spray the tops with olive oil and season lightly with garlic salt.

6. Place them in the air fryer at 400°F for 5 minutes then flip over and cook for and addition 5 minutes.

Notes: Can Bake in the oven at 375°F for 12 minutes and flip half way through cook time. You want the tops to be golden brown.
Can use Rotisserie chicken or Whole Chicken Breast (cooked and shredded) if preferred!

Bacon Cheeseburger Bombs

INGREDIENTS

1 lb ground beef

Bacon (crumbled)

1 cup shredded cheese

1 packet of Lipton© Beefy Onion Soup mix

Pepper

1 tbsp minced garlic

2-8ct. pack of Crescent Rolls

½ stick of butter

1 tsp garlic salt

1 tsp parsley

DIRECTIONS

1. Preheat oven to 375°F.
2. Cook ground beef and season with pepper, minced garlic and Lipton© Beefy Onion Soup mix.
3. Cook and crumble bacon, then combine ground beef and crumbled bacon together.
4. Lay out crescent roll and separate the triangles. Place a scoop of the meat mixture onto each triangle.
5. Place a small amount of shredded cheese on top of the meat mixture and close the crescent roll up, ensuring no meat or cheese is coming out.
6. Melt butter, garlic salt and parsley in a microwavable safe bowl.
7. Brush the top of each crescent roll with melted butter, garlic salt and parsley mixture.
8. Bake at 375°F for 12 minutes or until golden brown.
9. Serve and enjoy!

Notes: Can Air Fry as well!
Air fry at 350°F for 5-6 minutes until tops are golden brown.

Meatloaf Pinwheels

INGREDIENTS

1lb ground beef

1½ cups Italian breadcrumbs

½ yellow onions (diced)

1 large egg

1 tbsp minced garlic

1 tbsp Italian seasoning

½ cup ketchup

½ cup Texas Roadhouse© Gold Sauce (Can use BBQ Sauce)

Thick cut bacon

Crispy fried onions

GLAZE INGREDIENTS

⅓ Cup Texas Roadhouse© Gold Sauce (Can use BBQ Sauce)

⅓ cup ketchup

1 tbsp Worcestershire Sauce

2 tbsp brown sugar

DIRECTIONS

1. Preheat oven to 375°F.

2. In a large mixing bowl combine ground beef, Italian breadcrumbs, onion, egg, minced garlic, Italian seasoning, ketchup and Texas Roadhouse© Gold Sauce.

3. Lay thick cut bacon out one slice at a time and place ground beef mixture on to bacon slices in an even layer.

4. Roll up each bacon slice, placing a toothpick at the end to help hold it together.

5. Bake in the oven at 375°F for 35 minutes.

6. Top with glaze and crispy fried onions then cook for an additional 10 minutes.

GLAZE DIRECTIONS

1. In a bowl add all glaze ingredients and mix until well combined.

Stuffed Tenderloin

INGREDIENTS

1 pork tenderloin

Bacon

2 tbsp diced jalapenos

½ tbsp juice from the diced jalapenos

1 cup shredded cheese

1 block cream cheese (softened)

1 package of Ranch seasoning

Salt

Pepper

Garlic

Smoked paprika

DIRECTIONS

1. Preheat Oven to 400°F.
2. In a baking dish, lay bacon across the pan horizontally covering the entire pan.
3. Butterfly your pork tenderloin and season with salt, pepper, garlic and smoked paprika. Make sure you season both sides of your tenderloin.
4. In a small mixing bowl, combine the diced jalapenos, jalapeno juice, shredded cheese, cream cheese and Ranch seasoning. Ensure you mix the ingredients very well.
5. Take your cheese mixture and scoop into the center of the pork tenderloin. Close the tenderloin up the best you can and place it on top of the bacon in the baking dish.
6. Wrap the bacon tightly over the stuffed pork tenderloin.
7. Bake in oven at 400°F for 1 hour. Let rest for 5-7 minutes before slicing and enjoy!

Lazy Teriyaki Stir Fry

INGREDIENTS

½ yellow onion (sliced)

12oz bag broccoli florets (fresh)

12oz -8ct. Steak-umm© sliced steak

½ cup Teriyaki sauce

⅓ cup Sweet Thai Chili sauce

2 tbsp Kinder's© Grilled Veggie seasoning

2 tbsp steak seasoning

½ tbsp butter

2 cups white instant rice

2 cups water

Salt

Pepper

DIRECTIONS

1. Slice up onion and place in skillet with broccoli florets. Drizzle with olive oil and let steam on medium to low heat until softened. Season with Grilled Veggie seasoning.

2. In a separate skillet, place frozen steak with a drizzle of olive oil and season with steak seasoning. Chop the steak up in the skillet and let cook till browned.

3. Once the steak is browned, pour Teriyaki sauce and Sweet Thai Chilli sauce on top of the steak and combine well.

4. Combine the broccoli, onions and steak together. Let simmer for 3-4 mins on low to medium heat.

5. Cook instant white rice according to the instructions on the box, adding in the butter. Add salt and pepper to taste.

6. Assemble your plate - spoon on the white rice and place the meat mixture on the top.

7. Drizzle a little more of the Teriyaki sauce and enjoy!

Glazed Ham and Cheese

INGREDIENTS

2 rolls Crescent Dough sheet

16oz honey ham

8oz Swiss block cheese (Shred)

¼ cup mayonnaise

GLAZE INGREDIENTS

⅓ cup light brown sugar

4 tbsp butter

1 tbsp Worcestershire Sauce

1 tbsp minced garlic

1 tsp Creole seasoning

1 tsp oregano

1 tbsp mustard

DIRECTIONS

1. Preheat Oven to 375°F.

2. Shred Swiss block cheese.

3. Lay out one crescent dough sheet and spread mayonnaise on the dough.

4. Place ham over the mayonnaise in an even layer.

5. Spread shredded Swiss cheese in an even layer over the ham.

6. Lay your second can of crescent dough sheet over the cheese and press the bottom and top dough sheets together.

7. Top lightly with the glaze.

8. Bake in oven at 375°F for 12 minutes.

9. Flip over, then lightly glaze again and cook for an additional 12 minutes.

10. Slice into desired sizes and top with remaining glaze.

GLAZE DIRECTIONS

1. In a microwavable safe bowl, combine light brown sugar, butter, Worcestershire Sauce, minced garlic, Creole seasoning, oregano and mustard.

2. Melt in the microwave for 30 second intervals, until butter is fully melted and mix all ingredients together.

3. Brush onto the crescent dough sheet and enjoy!

Crock Pot

In this last chapter, you will find some of my favorite, and easiest slow cooker meals that are great for those busy adults. These recipes are good to put in the slow cooker in the morning, and let cook all day to be ready to eat when you get home.

Marry Me Chicken

INGREDIENTS

3-4 boneless/skinless chicken breasts

1 tbsp cornstarch

1 cup heavy whipping cream

½ cup chicken broth

1 tbsp minced garlic

2 tbsp onion powder

2 tbsp Italian seasoning

1 tbsp crushed red pepper flakes

1 tbsp oregano

2 tbsp fresh thyme (chopped)

1 cup sun dried tomatoes (Julienne cut with herbs)

5oz shredded Parmesan cheese

DIRECTIONS

1. Pour the heavy whipping cream, chicken broth and cornstarch into the slow cooker. Mix the ingredients together very well.

2. Place the chicken breast into the slow cooker and season with onion powder, Italian seasoning, crushed red pepper flakes, oregano, thyme and minced garlic.

3. Top the seasoned chicken breast with sun dried tomatoes (drain as much oil out of them as possible when removing from the jar) and shredded Parmesan cheese.

4. Cook on high for 4-5 hours or low for 6-7 hours.

5. Serve and enjoy!

Notes: Best served over mashed potatoes or buttered noodles!

Smothered Pork Chops

INGREDIENTS

6 boneless pork chops

2 tbsp Creole seasoning

1 tbsp minced garlic

1-10.5oz can Cream of Mushroom soup

1 packet of low sodium brown gravy

½ yellow onion (sliced)

DIRECTIONS

1. Place pork chops in the slow cooker, then season with Creole seasoning and minced garlic.
2. Slice onion.
3. In a separate bowl combine Cream of Mushroom, brown gravy mix and sliced onion.
4. Pour mixture on top of the pork chops.
5. Cook on high for 4 hours or low for 6 hours.

Notes: Onion is optional and best served over Mashed Potatoes!

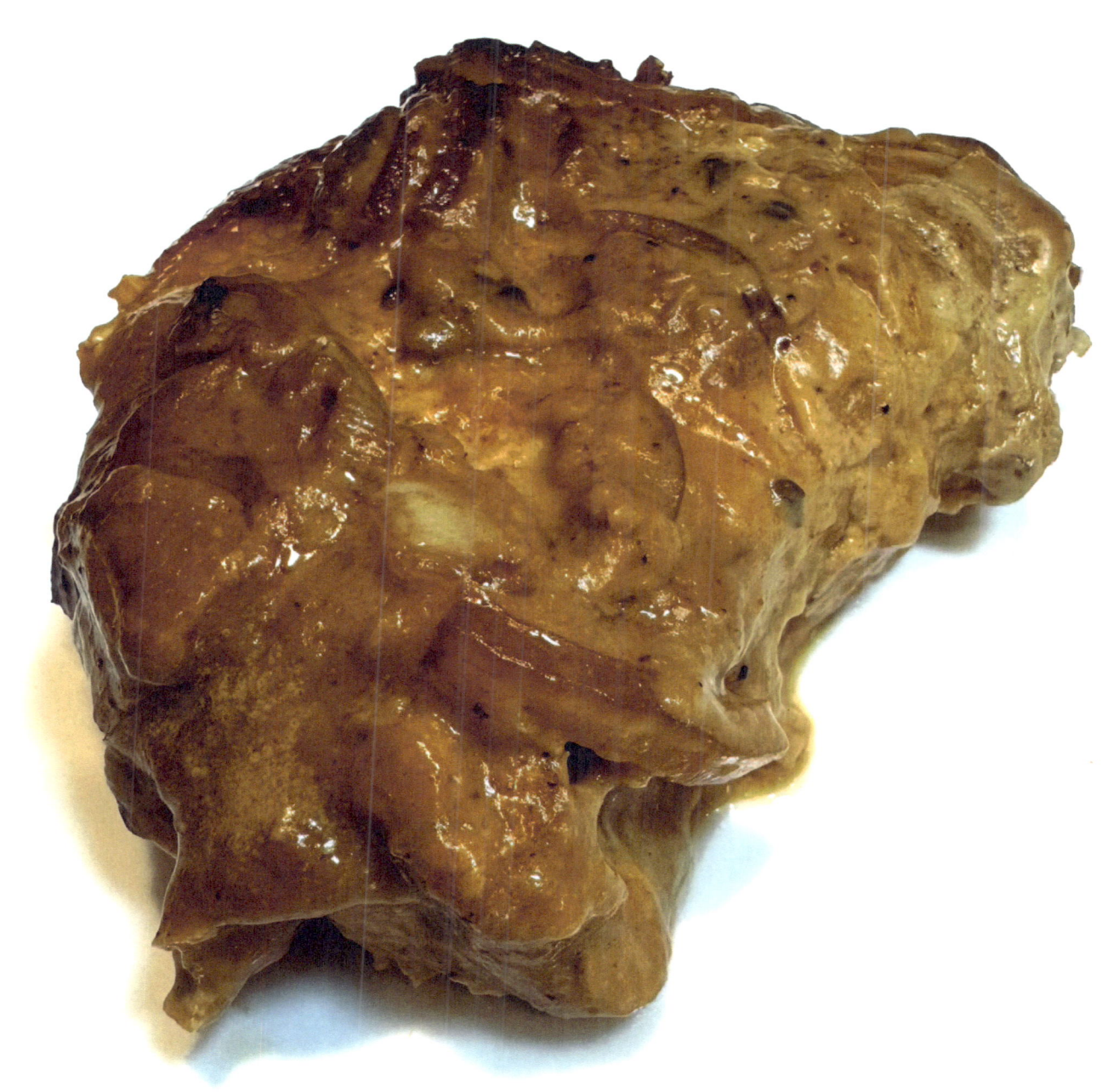

Chili

INGREDIENTS

1½ lbs ground beef

4-15oz cans mixed chili beans

1-10oz can Rotel

1 tbsp minced garlic

1 tbsp onion powder

1 tbsp pepper

1 cup beef broth

1 packet of Chili seasoning (hot or mild)

Shredded cheese

DIRECTIONS

1. Cook ground beef and season with minced garlic, onion powder and pepper.

2. Drain the grease from the ground beef and place in the slow cooker.

3. Pour Rotel, mixed chili beans, beef broth and packet of chili seasoning into the slow cooker with ground beef.

4. Mix until ingredients are well combined and cook on high for 4-5 Hours or low for 6-7 Hours.

5. Top with shredded cheese and enjoy!

Hot Honey Ribs

INGREDIENTS

1 rack of baby back ribs (pork or beef)

1 cup Buffalo sauce

1 cup honey

1 tbsp cornstarch

1 tbsp minced garlic

½ stick of butter (melted)

½ cup lemon juice

½ cup brown sugar

DIRECTIONS

1. Pull the membrane off the back of the ribs.
2. Slice up the ribs individually and place in the slow cooker.
3. In a separate small mixing bowl, melt down your butter and add in Buffalo sauce, honey, Cornstarch, minced garlic, lemon juice and brown sugar.
4. Mix the sauce together very well and pour over the top of the ribs in the slow cooker.
5. Ensure the sauce is coated over the top and sides of the ribs.
6. Cook on high for 4-5 hours or low for 6-8 hours.
7. Serve and enjoy!

Notes: If the sauce isn't thick enough add another spoonful of corn starch to the sauce and mix well. Let sit for 10-12 minutes and enjoy!
THIS IS NOT HOT! THE SAUCE IS A TANGY, SWEET FLAVOR!

Rotel Chicken

INGREDIENTS

3-4 boneless/skinless chicken breasts

1lb Box of spaghetti noodles

1-10oz can of Rotel (drained)

1-10.5oz can of Cream of Mushroom with Roasted Garlic soup

1-22oz can of Cream of Chicken soup

1 tbsp minced garlic

1 block of cream cheese

Salt

Pepper

Garlic salt

Creole seasoning (optional)

DIRECTIONS

1. Place chicken breasts in slow cooker and season with salt, pepper, garlic salt, minced garlic and Creole seasoning.
2. Put cream cheese, Rotel (drained), Cream of Mushroom with Roasted Garlic and Cream of Chicken on top of the chicken breasts.
3. Cook on high for 4-5 hours or low for 6-7 hours.
4. Cook spaghetti noodles according to directions on the box.
5. Once chicken is completely cooked, shred.
6. Place the cooked/drained spaghetti noodles into the slow cooker with the shredded chicken and mix together well.
7. Serve and enjoy!

Notes: Take it up a notch and add shredded cheese to the top before serving!

Cheesy Beef Tortellini

INGREDIENTS

1½ lb ground beef

1-36oz bag of cheese Tortellini

1-22oz jar of Roasted Garlic Parmesan Alfredo Sauce

1-22oz jar of Marinara Sauce

1 cup heavy whipping cream

½ block cream cheese

1 tbsp Italian seasoning

1 tbsp Creole seasoning

1 tbsp minced garlic

1 cup Mozzarella cheese

Parmesan cheese

DIRECTIONS

1. Cook ground beef and season with Italian seasoning, Creole seasoning and minced garlic.

2. Place cooked ground beef, bag of Cheese Tortellini, jar of Roasted Garlic Parmesan Alfredo Sauce, jar of Marinara Sauce, heavy whipping cream, cream cheese and Mozzarella in a slow cooker.

3. Mix together very well and cook on high for 4-5 hours or low for 6-7 hours.

4. Top with Parmesan and serve!

Hash Brown Chicken

INGREDIENTS

2lb Bag of Southern Style Hash Browns (Frozen)

3-4 Boneless/Skinless Chicken Breasts (Cubed)

16oz Heavy Whipping Cream

2 Tbsp Olive Oil

1 Tbsp Minced Garlic

2 Tbsp Onion Powder

2 Tbsp Garlic Powder

2 Tbsp Smoked Paprika

2 Tbsp Italian Seasoning

2 Cups Shredded Cheese

3 Cups Bacon (Crumbled or Bacon Bits)

Salt (To Taste)

Pepper (To Taste)

DIRECTIONS

1. Cube your chicken breasts into bite size pieces and place in the crockpot.

2. Place the rest of the ingredients into the slow cooker except for 1 cup of bacon.

3. Cook on high for 3-4 hours or low for 5-6 hours.

4. Top with remaining bacon and enjoy!

Velveeta© Mac Pasta

INGREDIENTS

1½ lb ground beef

½ yellow onions (diced)

1 tbsp minced garlic

1 tbsp Creole seasoning

Pepper (to taste)

2 tbsp Kinder's© The Blend

2 tbsp smoked paprika

1 -10.5oz can of Cream of Chicken with Herb soup

1 -10oz can Rotel

1 block cream cheese

1-16oz block Velveeta©

16oz Bowtie pasta

1½ Cups beef broth

DIRECTIONS

1. Cook ground beef with diced onion and minced garlic.

2. Cook pasta according to the directions on the package.

3. Place cooked/drained pasta noodles and cooked ground beef into the slow cooker.

4. Season with Creole seasoning, Kinder's© The Blend, pepper and smoked paprika.

5. Add Can of Cream of Chicken with Herb, Rotel, cream cheese, Velveeta© and beef broth into the slow cooker and mix all ingredients until well combined.

6. Cook in the slow cooker on high for 2 hours or low for 4 hours.

BBQ Meatballs

INGREDIENTS

1- 3lb bag of frozen homestyle meatballs

2 cups brown sugar

2 cups BBQ sauce

1 cup grape jelly

1 cup honey

DIRECTIONS

1. Place meatballs, brown sugar, BBQ sauce, grape jelly and honey in the slow cooker.
2. Mix ingredients well and cook on high for 4-5 hours or low for 6-7 hours.
3. Serve and enjoy!

Notes: Best served over Mash Potatoes.
To thicken up the sauce, make a Cornstarch Slurry which is equal parts, cornstarch and water. Mix together and pour over meatballs and combine well. Let sit for 7 minutes before serving if you add slurry mix!

Loaded Baked Potato Soup

INGREDIENTS

2lb Bag of Southern style hash browns (frozen)

22.6oz can of Cream of Chicken soup

1 block of cream cheese

4 cups bacon (crumbled) or bacon bits

1 package Dry Ranch seasoning

Shredded cheese

32oz box of chicken broth

2 tbsp onion powder

2 tbsp pepper

Green onion

Sour cream

DIRECTIONS

1. In a slow cooker place the full 2lb bag of frozen has browns, Cream of Chicken, Cream Cheese, Dry Ranch seasoning, 2 cups of cooked/crumbed Bacon (can use bacon bits), entire box of chicken broth, onion powder and pepper.

2. Cook on low for 6-7 hours or high for 4-5 hours.

3. Top with shredded cheese, crumbled bacon, green onion and sour cream.

4. Serve and enjoy!

Million Dollar Chicken

INGREDIENTS

1 lb chicken breasts (boneless and skinless)

1 block cream cheese (softened)

2 cups of shredded cheese

Bacon

1 packet of Ranch seasoning

½ cup mayonnaise

Creole seasoning

Garlic salt

Salt

Pepper

Onion powder

2 cups green onions

DIRECTIONS

1. Place chicken breasts into a slow cooker and season both sides with Creole seasoning, garlic salt, pepper, salt and onion powder.

2. In a small mixing bowl combine the softened cream cheese, mayonnaise and packet of Ranch seasoning.

3. Pour the cheese mixture on top of the chicken breasts, ensuring its spread out evenly.

4. Top with shredded cheese and green onion.

5. Cook on low for 6-7 hours or high for 4-5.

6. Serve and enjoy!

Notes: Best Served Over Mash Potatoes!